The Arches

The Arches

TONY CURTIS & JOHN DIGBY

seren

seren is the book imprint of
Poetry Wales Press Ltd
Wyndham Street, Bridgend, Wales

ISBN 1-85411-236-8
1-85411-237-6 pbk

A CIP record for this title is available from the British Library

*The publisher acknowledges the financial support of the
Arts Council of Wales*

Printed in Plantin by The Cromwell Press Ltd, Trowbridge

The Arches

I

There are always two ways
of looking at a thing.

Botticelli the lighthouse keeper
stares over the rocks' spume and flash
until the crash of waves
curl to form a shell
she grows from.
Modest, voluptuous tresses
folded around her.

The gulls, the bawdy gulls
screech in the angry, randy air.

Inside, the other man
does all he can
to placate the raucous sea.
He has thrown amphorae
to the waves.
        'What do you want?
What am I to do?'
he calls.

With his knife
he has sliced away one skin, one face.
New, young again, he feels strong,
strong enough to jump through the rough arch,
through the mirage of her
and strike out for the lighthouse,
the attainable lighthouse.

II

Inside the second arch
the jugs are all in place,
where they have been placed.

Full fathom five the senses live.
The pearls have been plucked
from Liberty's eyes.

She's wrecked so far
from Ellis Island
and clutches to the dated tablet
like a lifesaver.

III

The King's humour
bodes ill.

The Archbishop, as slow as an ox,
has blundered in front of expediency
with his plodding dogma
and dull sermonizing.
The air is foul with incense
and the dust of cathedrals.
His reverence is trussed and bound
for the abattoir.

The Fool's displeased the court –
his lute's broken. Now
he sings a different song
and is unaccompanied.

Wise counsel has lost its head
and paid for it at the block.
The court and the country
holds its breath.

IV

From over the snow mountains they come.
Each night, I beat them back,
crush and shape them
on the anvil of my fear.

The whirr of their wings like a buzz-saw.
Their blank, totem faces.

It was always their land,
but the sky was ours.
The distant choppers like the pulsing of our blood
was proof we could survive it all

It is pure now when it returns,
the sharp, clear snow
that has settled over everything
like a shroud.

V

When they have all gone.
After the shouting and the noise.
I go to the arch and look out.

The kind old gardener digs near
the beehives.
His wheelbarrow has tipped over.
I could shout to him,
but I'll wait. Grass will grow
through the spokes of its wheel.
Weeds will close their fists on the handles.

There is a garden wall high enough
to keep the gardener, the shrubs, the beans
inside. But not too high so that
– I shall call them giraffes –
a giant could crane his neck
over and chew the sappy green leaves.

The gardener levers the tines of his fork
through the earth. Stones, worms,
roots will be lifted into the light.

VI

The whole world spread below me –
the quilt of sown fields, the stitched hedges,
the clustered trees, the river's ribbon
all seen through clouds I could taste.

The engine of my flight whirred like wasps
after a climbing boy.

And then the branch of my belief snapped.
I fell back through the arch of our desiring
where the grinning idiot,
our earth-bound country cousin,
waits, always, with his brush
to sweep it all away.

VII

Each night I takes out
one stone –
no more – one stone is enough.

Eyes only
is the rule.

She dances, slow like:
it might be a fan,
it might be a hat,
it might be, say, an umbrella.

I dare say there's a skill to it –
a pretty little thing with her hair
pinned up from a face it pains me to look on.
A thing of beauty, you might say,
a cause of pain in the not having of her.

They pay, handsomely, those outside.
For the viewing of her skin,
her jugs like fruit,
her face turned aside, the curl of her eyebrows,
the line of her cheeks and nose,
the curve of her belly,
the delicious split fig of her.

And when it is finished,
I fits back the stone, shuts
out the light and stands with my arms
aching like I done a day's work,
like severed limbs.

VIII

Under the sickle moon
I shall be Alice
and follow the svelte rabbit
out of the ruined tower
passing to the arch where, huge,
I find the medicine and spoon.

A spoonful, a spoonful.
It would be so easy here
and now, the stars at my back,
the rustling trees with their advice,
the moon a slice of used light.

The music of leaves washes through me.
I know that there is something immense
I must do. Something.

There is a device on the handle of the spoon
that the craftsman has cleverly engraved.
An apple ripe on the branch
which a hand should close around.

IX

Do twins share the same nightmare?
It is three, the hour of depths,
and they are woken
by the crashing of a jar.

A man like none they have ever seen
– father, uncle, soldier –
has lifted a pear above his shoulders
and makes as if to throw that huge fruit.

There the dream freezes. It is absurd.
A pun.
Do the pair of brothers compose such a scene?
And why? Or is it one dreaming of one. And one.

X

If she would be a fisher
of men
let her cast from the rocks
and try her hook and line
to the seaward and the land.
Amphorae, caught, raised and then broken,
litter the rocks of dream.

In some room he lies –
stiff Christ in deposition,
his scarred hands and feet,
his wounded heart.

Of this she knows nothing.
For she has the skies,
the prominence of rocks,
the sea with its pillar of rain
moving like a curtain.

Soon the evening will turn chill
and she will lift up her skirts,
return to the house where
she finds there is an exquisite
vase the maid has broken
and where the gardener,
hearing her scream, has left
against the kitchen wall
his careless spade.

XI

Vipers!
Low-bellied sliders,
asps, boas, striped and scaled strikers,
full-muscled, thick as hawsers –
these shall I summon with my wand,
my pen.

From the height of my age,
all that I have achieved,
such mosaiced coils,
diamonded ropes I will offer
as necklaces for my critics.
All this – and lightning!

XII

The ladies of the seashore
seal their wishes in jugs
they cast to the sea
that float, briefly in the waves.

The sea grows rough and none
will ever be found on a distant shore
by a man hungry for love and the words
of a woman's imagination.

He is cold and the night weighs
on him like a damp cloak.
His wife coughs and his children
have the eyes of yesterday's fish.

The ladies of the seashore
watch the sea turning white with anger.
They dream of captains of the world
who know its taste is salt.

XIII

This is not Noah
who, left stranded on a dry mountain crag,
takes his oar and rocks the craft
which teeters over the ocean of air.

Better by far
to drink the rare, refinement of air
and contemplate heights, depths,
the storm that will surely come.

Look around, the sky
with its bubbling, dark clouds
promises turbulence enough
to float you out of this crashed world.

XIV

Overboard –
the wet deck, the shaky rail
the river in spate
– overboard!

The passengers crowd to the side
and scream at the churning waters.

This is the dream of the steamer
that paddles each night through the arches
of the Alms-House on Blackwell's Island.

Where John Bard, painter of the Hudson fleet
– the rich man's yachts, the honest cargomen,
the *Clermont*, the *Alida*, *Spartan*
the boats on wheels –
is dying in crazy confusion.

Far from his paints and brushes,
far from someone he thinks
might be his brother, James,
who does not call,
who has not called since 1850,
these six years,
so how could he be?

XV

On, on, further on
into the dark continent
where it is our God-given duty
to bring light.

Through the rocks and foliage
I have climbed to the source
always the source, the beginning,
the sweet source of the great shining lake,
the slow, soupy river
that becomes the sea.

For these people are naked
without knowledge. Savages,
they live by water but have no interest
in from whence it may come.
Sweet Jesus.

The women perform their carrying.
Dark creatures, they come from a darkness
which our naming of things shall unveil for them.
But for their darkness
this could be an Eden
and she an Eve, though fallen.

These hot nights I am disturbed
by dreams. She holds aloft water,
she holds the milks of life
and the juices from which all
the continents grow.

XVI

On the seventh night
again the vessel placed beneath the tree.
Clear of the clouds, chill stars
promise frost, the withering of leaves.

Since the tree grew in the middle of the road
there has been no fruit
and the townspeople
have tightened into themselves.

Lives pass by
on the other side of lives.
Memory is an ancient statue broken
in the classical manner.

Perfection is incomplete.
The citizens are nervous behind their shutters
and the deserted road is both threatening
and the quiet they would always have wished.

Cold moonlight brushes the houses –
it dreams through each hour of the night
and will not easily be propitiated.
The seven vessels, holding nothing, must be broken.

XVII

This was not meant to be.
I thought that we were on lines
to some kind of place together,
some heights we both could see.

But there, like a mammoth,
was the tusked imperative of common sense.
Derailed, a tangled mess, I felt upended.
And then we stopped using words.

Into the icy quiet of our aftermath,
only the sound of your chair creaking
as you bent to pick up the pieces
of a broken coffee cup.

XVIII

I shall stay at my desk.
I have listened to the tales,
I have sat quietly, away from the centre,
while these men tell of their strange lands,
seas like magenta mountains,
mountains like heavens, the endless rivers,
the impenetrable dark forests,
the fruits of the ripe jungle.

But God has meant me for France.
Where I live I shall die.
These unnatural flights on hot air
are hubris, the coloured re-telling
of horned horses, flying fish.
Tall tales and nonsense.
As their baskets lift up them up and away
into their unrecorded deaths
I shall lift my pen
and journey by sitting still.

XIX

Adam the apple gatherer –
for a week of myths
he has walked into her dreams.
Over the sea, over the rocks,
under the shooting stars.

He is perfect
as a statue is perfect,
his body smooth as marble,
though the apple twig he carries
is precarious and absurd.

Clothed and jewelled,
pillowed in repose, she
is the guardian of the fruit,
of the jugs of wine.
He is a love-lorn boy
and will not judge her.

XX

Mama and I went behind the arches
to change me for the bathing.
'There,' she said, 'Be gone!'
to the excited birds that wheeled
before us as if sensing food.

She had smoothed oil on me
against the sun and wind
and the salt of the sea.

I saw only flying boy-hungry creatures
from the beginnings of time
that smelling my oiled body
were tasting me with their wet eyes.

The moon strangely in the same sky
as the low sun
grew large and like some huge stone
began to roll towards us, quite filling the sky.

'Hold me, Mama!' I cried,
though uttered not a word
that she could hear, 'Hold me
against the moon,
against all the creatures of the sky.
Against the salty hunger of the sea.'

XXI

In the Hotel Ty-Mad it is quiet
but for the creak of floorboards in the room below.
In Treboul harbour the boats knock
one against the other.
He has smoked the last of his hoard
and has taken to eating the dross.

This is Kit Wood's opium dream:
all his oils and canvases
are not more to life
than a stiff photographist's posed
woman disembarking,
the wind blurring for ever her scarf and shawl
so that she seems as if taking flight
out of his frame.

She wavers between
her pet dog on the quayside
and the souvenir amphorae they peddle
along this coast.

She will be gone before the light
can work to fix an image in his box
and already the four Chinese acrobats
descend from an empty sky
like some apocalypse.

They swing from the belly of the dragon
and will take away each one –
woman, photographist, dog, the gang-plank itself –
leaving nothing but silence
and the empty vessels.

XXII

High in the peaks
above the snowline
has appeared a tower
from which a prophet calls.
His outstretched arms are reaching for the world.

Here the prayers are pure and principled
in the rare and clean air,
though the words travel
like knives down over the snow,
the lichened rocks, the grazing slopes,
over the desert to the seas
where, in time, whales beach themselves
helplessly, knowing no reason.

This was ever the way –
from the high clarity
the waves of confusion
turn to the words
that lead us astray.

XXIII

After the dwarf gladiators,
the bladed chariot races,
the monkey crucifixion,
today the Emperor puts on
the spotted horse.

From the four corners
of the greatest empire
the world will ever know
new wonders are brought for our show.

The armoured bull.
The white deer and the pink.
The giant cats that tame men.

And now the spotted horse
is slung into the arena –
its spindle legs akimbo,
its stretched neck, nose
balancing an amphora full,
it is said, with myrrh,
spice, frankincense,
it would take a man
his life to earn.

Oh, and we gasp,
we cry. Everything
is in the balance.

XXIV

These afternoons Stella takes me
out for the air.
Past winter, the ice holds
for much of the spring.
We go further each day,
for she says I grow lighter
and that pushing me is no more than walking.
Perhaps she is right; or perhaps
it is that she grows stronger.

When the sun breaks
the ice hits one like a cold desert's glare.

As we go further the trees and the house
disappear and we are truly
in a desert. Back there
the dog waits. He will bark and jump
when we re-appear.

These afternoons are my freedom in the crisp air
where everything becomes clear.
Why then do I feel this burden?

And why is there this weight on me
like the grip of many arms?
From which, I fear, I shall
make no escape.

XXV

And then there was
one amphora
one gull
in the sanctuary
looking back
at the colonies of birds
on a massive, unreal rock –
generations on generations,
the tons of guano,
the throb of each crevice-clutched egg
smooth and worn as an oval room
in which one might fashion
a decorated arch.

One amphora.
One gull.
One cannot imagine flight.

The Genesis of The Arches Collage Series
John Digby

So much the rather thou Celestial Light
Shine inward, and the mind through all her powers
Irradiate, there plant eyes, all mist from thence
Purge and disperse, that I may see and tell
Of things invisible to moral sight

John Milton, *Paradise Lost* III, 52-55

'My Father's mansion has many rooms,' repeated Sister Thompson, the nun who taught my first class in infants school. That remark startled, astonished and bewildered me. As a five-year-old it changed my life. From that moment I started off on an imaginary voyage that has never ended. How many rooms were there? How large were they? What shape were they? Who or what occupied them? I had this vague image, a childish construction of a house in which countless rooms manufactured themselves to infinity.

Ah, Sister Thompson, 'noli me tangere', but you did! I owe a great deal to you – for your sentence was the spark that set fire to my imagination, and out of the misery that you inflicted on me it rose phoenix-like, voyaging into worlds of its own. All day I struggled, trying to understand and to visualize these rooms and the shape of this implied mansion. Even in the playground among the boisterous children, I was deaf to their laughter and ignored their games, drifting alone, musing, pondering this mansion of many rooms.

Despite my struggles, I did not ask Sister Thompson for any further illumination, as I found her to be a formidable character. In truth, I was frightened of this wizened creature draped in black who ruled the class with a twelve inch steel ruler and a caustic tongue. Many times I felt that ruler slap across the back of my left hand in order to correct me, that is to say, force me to write with my right hand. I shed tears with another who was left-handed –

Henry Ford. Ah, Henry, I wonder if you too recall the sultry tears stinging our flushed cheeks as our left hands tingled with pain from the punitive ruler! I hope, Henry, that you too benefitted from this inflicted misery!

Still, I owe a great deal to you Sister Thompson. You gave birth to my imagination, but though you declared that 'my Father's mansion has many rooms', I could never picture this sinister figure draped in black having a father. That was way beyond my comprehension, I who was also without a father.

I pestered my grandmother about Sister Thompson's remark. She wisely or unwisely gave me no interpretation 'You must think about it yourself,' she offered. And so I did. Even during the Second World War when the Luftwaffe were flying overhead at night bombing London I awakened in the early morning light to gaze at the cracks of the bedroom ceiling, searching for those rooms as if they could be entered through those thin white crevices. To find these rooms was not an escape, but a genuine desire to locate and see inside this mythical mansion. Like the wife of Bluebeard, I was willing to take any risk to explore and open each and every door and if empty to fill that room with my imaginary beings and scenes.

Many of those scenes were occupied with characters that were birds. I'm told that as an infant while being wheeled through parks in a baby carriage by my mother and/or grandmother, I pointed to birds – sparrows, starlings, pigeons, ducks and the swans that glided across the ornamental ponds – the only beings that excited me as a child. Even before I could speak I was told I was crazy about animal life, especially birds. Therefore, in order to pursue my childhood obsession to be an aviculturist or ornithologist, the only option open to me was the London Zoo. As a mere fifteen-year-old I became a keeper at the London Zoo in the small bird house, a request I made even before I left school. There, unconsciously, I wandered into that *mansion of many rooms*. I finally arrived.

My first job in the small bird house was the cleaning of the 'backs and fronts' of a series of seventeen aviaries. The 'backs', as they were affectionately called by the elder, more experienced staff, were the winter quarters of the tropical birds; the 'fronts' were the large flight cages open to the public view. There was nothing seemingly magical about the structure of those aviaries, but keeping them clean was one of the happiest times of my life. Although working in the bird house never once brought back to mind Sister Thompson's mansion of many rooms, I had indeed taken my place in that mansion as keeper. Even today, I look back at those days and consider that I had glimpsed into paradise. It was a peaceable kingdom that embraced worlds. Every aviary was the same, only smaller or larger depending on its residents. In one cage I visited Africa, in another Australia, Europe, the Americas and so on. Thus I was, as I went from aviary to aviary, voyaging in my imagination from continent to continent, each an Eden with its fountain and foliage inhabited by its own collection of birds. And in some cases, birds from different continents lived together in one aviary that was a perfectly magical kingdom corresponding to no place on earth that I have known.

In this ideal world I knew I was happy, for the reason that I was working with my obsession, the love of birds. I could not quite place my finger on it, but at times I experienced a strange sensation while I was working. There were brief moments among the cries, the calls, and notes of the birds when I felt myself somewhere else, in a future time. Now and then I saw glimpses of myself, so I supposed, as a much older person in landscapes that were totally foreign to me. They flashed in front of me at such a speed that the images appeared too blurred to comprehend in any way whatsoever, except to realize that they had appeared. It was almost a mystical experience. I put it down to just sheer happiness.

Alas, after two years I was transferred to another bird house, the pheasantry. Although I loved that house as well, I did not experience the same emotions as I did in the small bird house. After six years, the longest job I ever held, I quit the London Zoo and drifted from office job to office job. They put me, by contrast, in places of many rooms that were not mansions. I separated myself from these places in spirit and began searching – perhaps for what I had lost – in the writing of poetry, my restless spirit seeking something way beyond my grasp. Looking back on them now, my poems seem filled with the birds I left in the

London Zoo.

It wasn't until later when I discovered surrealism, that my restless spirit was somewhat appeased. I started to make collages, at first to illustrate my poems and to depict some of the magical encounters of the imagination. But I was still far removed from that almost visionary experience that I sometimes had as a youth while working in the small bird house.

It was about seven or eight years ago while I was working in my studio that I happened to glance up from my work and witness an extraordinary sight that brought me back to that time. There in front of me, looking out from my studio into the next room, I saw myself as a youth of fifteen years working in the small bird house. The encounter was beyond the surreal; it was so real as to be a mystical experience – I looked at myself as a youth and as a youth I looked back at myself. Our eyes met. It was as if we were strangers. There was no recognition between us.

I have always had the ability to switch my imagination on and off, and after that experience I could conjure up the scene at will. The only way I can describe it is "pleasantly haunting". At times it became so real that I could have stretched out my hand and touched myself as a youth. I never did, however, because I could see myself – the youth – too intent at work to be disturbed.

And yet I wanted something from him – from myself. I needed to express this situation, but not in words – visually. I wanted to do it in some oblique manner. But how? I decided not to invent anything that might possibly express it, as it might appear forced. I had to discover it, or let it discover itself.

About a year later I was working, for an exhibition in New York, on a group of collages that I call 'beside themselves'. These are images in which figures step outside themselves to reveal other scenes in silhouette that allude to their inner life. The concept is something like me seeing myself as a youth, and so I was not surprised when that incident returned to me at the moment that I happened upon a nineteenth-century illustration of a room entitled, 'Torre de las Infantas, Alhambra'.

In a flash everything came back to me, people, places, scenes, sounds, smells, voices, birdnotes; incidents from the small bird house raced into my head like a swiftly running newsreel from the days when I was a 'boy' cleaning the aviaries. The whole series of the collages were completed. I needed only to start work, for the actual images hung in front of me like Samuel Palmer's fruit in his painting, 'The Magic Apple Tree'.

What was it about the illustration of a room entitled, 'Tour de las Infantas, Alhambra', that sparked this sudden rush of creativity? As I look at the illustration now, I realize that the female figure sitting and holding a book in her hands vaguely recalled Sister Thompson. In a flash I knew that was the scene I was searching for. It was perfect. It was an archway at the Alhambra through which the viewer could see a scene in the background. It reminded me absolutely of 'backs and fronts', the aviaries from the London small bird house. Each approach was the same, the same aviary, but each back room was different. As I wandered from room to room I experienced something different each time. I was determined to use the Alhambra print to finally come to terms with that perplexing remark about the mansion with many rooms. By using this print, I could express a place in which the approach to the room would always be the same, but if I removed the back or the inner scene and replaced it with one from my imagination, then I could express the visionary feeling and experience that I had as a child while working at the small bird house.

As a series, *The Arches* go beyond the single experience that made Sister Thompson's mansion of many rooms real to me. Here I was able, as an architect in paper, to collage my understanding of the idea that 'my Father's mansion has many rooms.' I, myself, am the child of my imagination, and every time I go to the drawing board to create another work, I am adding a room on my house. In this series I have used certain symbols to emphasize that point. The repeat pattern of the ever changing chambers of the imagination derive, of course, from the 'backs and fronts' of those aviaries in which I literally found myself. The arch is the vista (and its limitations) through which I can see and imagine. The jug is the vessel of the imagination. As much as I use up, more is delivered to me. It contains water, life, ideas, images – whatever the viewer imagines to be within. The scenes themselves often allude to the characters I remember from my days in the small bird house as well as characters from history and beliefs. I hesitate to say religions because I am not religious, but belief in the spirit of the imagination is what carries my work forward. There are also contrasts, ironies, comedies and tragedies, because human life has all these components. And, of course, there are birds because for me they are the quintessential triggers of my imagination, and I owe them everything.

Meeting At The Arches
Tony Curtis

When John Digby rang me from Long Island in 1994 to suggest this collaboration I was both intrigued and puzzled. I had known John since the late 1970s as a poet and collagist. I had enjoyed his Statue of Liberty book from 1976 and had published some of my poems in anthologies which John and his wife Joan had edited and illustrated in the 1980s in New York.

Over the phone the Arches idea was difficult for me to visualise, but I knew that John would not have called without having thought out the proposal. As a poet, I am not often commissioned and do not often have to work to deadlines or under instruction. However, John's idea was a challenge and I immediately agreed to write poems to the first selection of collages he was to send. Of course, when they arrived – six or eight at first – I was sure that I could be provoked, persuaded and inspired to engage with the images and ideas of the collagist with words of my own.

I began as a poet in 1965 as a student at Swansea University, or at least I began to regard myself as a poet; it took a little longer for others to regard me as a poet. In my postgraduate year there I won the student poetry competition submitting a sequence of six short poems based on Picasso's 'Blue' and 'Pink' period paintings from the early years of the century. So, the strategy of seeding words and growing poems out of visual images was developed very early on in my work as a poet. In the 1970s and 1980s I wrote poems based on the photographs of Les Krim and published them as the 'Deerslayers' sequence; also, I began to respond to the work of the great American figurative painter Andrew Wyeth, producing eight poems which appeared in collections and the Tate Gallery anthology *Voices from the Gallery* edited by Dannie and Joan Abse. Over the years poems have come from a number of artists and sources: the American photographer O. Winston Link, painters such as Augustus John, William Orpen, Kyffin Williams, Munch and Graham Sutherland, the sculptor

Rodin and the printmaker Gertrude Hermes.

I must stress that I don't regard this as in any way plagiarism, or second-hand creativity: there are notable traditions of fresh responses to the work of others in music, literature and art – Vaughan Williams's 'Variation on a theme by Thomas Tallis' is one of the great evocations of the English landscape and spirit; Benjamin Britten's 'Peter Grimes', 'Billy Budd' and 'War Requiem' are interpretations of the work of the poets Crabbe and Wilfred Owen and the novelist Herman Melville. Remember W.H. Auden's 'Musée des Beaux Arts'. Nearly all opera and jazz compositions owe their being to the work of another, while ballet, theatre and film are of necessity collaborative ventures. The Arches project is based therefore on a natural cooperation between collagist and poet; particularly as the collagist is himself a published poet and the poet is as avid an art collector and commentator as his limited budget and knowledge will allow.

I first came across John Digby's work in the small, but influential, poetry magazine *Kayak* edited and run by George and Marjorie Hitchcock from Santa Cruz in California. They had generously hosted me for a week in 1978 when I was visiting America on a Rotary International sponsored visit. *Kayak* was produced in their huge and rambling house where, it seemed, they were hosts to a succession of writers on West Coast reading or promotional tours – Margaret Atwood was a guest during my short stay. The magazine was basic in its production values, but outstanding in terms of the poets it published: Gary Snyder, Charles Simic, Robert Bly and others. Between poems George inserted odd-ball nineteenth-century engravings, roughly collaged together and supplementing or complementing the underlying surreal angle of the poems and prose-poems. The effect of each issue was weird and wonderful, a breath of fresh air to a British reader. George and Marjorie spoke of the English poet John Digby who had stayed with them for some months shortly before. I should meet him, they said. A few years later I did and we have corresponded regularly ever since and hosted each other in Oyster Bay, Long Island and Barry in Wales.

John's commitment to the art of the surreal extends back through the last three decades. His collections of poetry from

Anvil Press in London and his inclusion in *The Penguin Book of English and American Surreal Poetry* underline the strange originality of his poetic vision; it is no surprise therefore that John Digby the self-taught collagist continues in that vein. The slicing of reality reveals by startling juxtapositions the possibilities of a deeper truth, closer to our dreams and by conventional means harder to access. In responding to John's Arches images I was likewise encouraged to move in and out of character and period and perspective, and I had used these strategies, in my war poems particularly, over the years. Of course, the reader will be able to discern re-occuring preoccupations or themes across and along the sequence. After all, the central and underpinning image of the arches themselves, the single arch of the template, sets up the possibility of exploring the dichotomy of inside/outside, of then/now, of me/them, of real and surreal, of fact and imagination.

I worked on these poems over a period of almost four years; sometimes putting pen to paper immediately after opening a package; sometimes producing more than one poem in draft at a sitting; sometimes putting the image aside and returning to it time and time again to tease out what it meant to me. At no point did John and I discuss the matter or form of each of the arch's image; our transatlantic calls and letters were exclusively concerned with the practical details of the project as it became more complex – individual poems and collages in poetry magazines, a book proposal, a slide and tape version at a campus festival in the University of Glamorgan, the idea of doing this as a video, and then, more recently, the decision to produce a CD-rom version with the book. I don't remember our agreeing to this procedure, but it must have seemed the best way to both engage with each other's imaginations and to preserve our individuality. Obviously, none of my poems would have come into being without John's images, though the concerns and – who knows? – some of the tropes could have been born in different places. Obviously, what we each produced as the series extended must have been involved in the following images and poems. But once it became clear, and this happened very early on, that we were both open to the possibilities and consequences of the collaboration, the Arches project was certainly going to lead to something different and interesting.

Tim Whitehead became involved in the project in the final year. Tim's wife Linda has been one of my M.A. in Writing distance-learning students and I was delighted to be able to invite Tim as a creative guest performer and lecturer to the campus. He is a fine musician and composer who brings a depth and sensitivity to everything he does, both as a soloist, leader of his quartet and improviser. His commitment to extending the bounds of British jazz and his proven powers to respond to place and mood in his location-inspired compositions made him in my eyes and ears an artist I'd thought I would love to work with. The vision and generosity of the Arts Council of Wales made that possible. In the early days I had joked with John about 'The Arches – the book, film and musical'!

The Arches can be taken at several levels and in several different ways: it is a book of illustrated poems; it is a book of collages with poetic improvisations; it is a performance tool; it is the catalogue to an art exhibition; it is an opportunity for the readers/users to interact through their PC in order to create their own images and words. The Arches started out as John Digby's; they became mine too, now they are yours to take forward.

Acknowledgements

Some of these poems and images have appeared in *Planet, Poetry Wales, The Rialto* and *Scintilla.*